HOW TO BAKE YOUR HEARTS

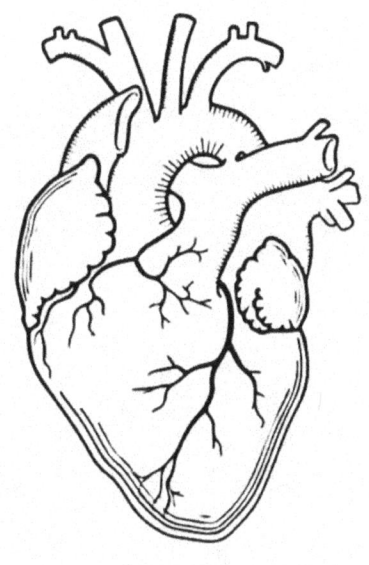

EVA LIUKINEVICIUTE

How to Bake Your Hearts ©2022 by **Eva Liukineviciute**. Published in the United States by Vegetarian Alcoholic Press, Inc. Not one part of this work may be reproduced without expressed written consent from the author. For more information, please write to V.A. Press, 643 South 2nd Street, Milwaukee, WI 53204

Metamorpho 32

Marcid 33

Choking 34

You Can't Shoot Ten Rabbits at Once 35

Verdure 36

Tossing 37

Entr'acte 38

Mother 39

Wishes 40

Cleaved, Softening Beaks 41

There is No Such Thing as Soft Violence 42

I Have a Pain in Our Teeth 43

Godnonsensical 44

Arcadia 45

The Sea-Foam Crown 46

To Glow 47

Contents:

Entre 5

Christening 6

Arterial 7

Floating 8

Liquid Fingernails 9

Borderling 10

Naif 11

Vous Serez Ma Proie 12

Mon Petit Chou 13

Atropa Belladonna 14

Over-Adequate 15

Viridis 16

Forest Bathing 17

Fairy Tales 18

Crab Fishing 19

Nothing is to be Mine; Everything Ours 20

Mére Vampire 21

Mére Mal 22

Alice 23

Ephialtes 24

Stockholm 25

Red Lettuce 26

Chorus 27

Bloodlines 28

Suivez-Moi. Je Vous Attendais 29

Lore 30

Feral in the Woods 31

Entre

Behind each bare step into softening mud, conifer trees
fold over themselves in languid origami; miniature
cranes and boats occluding my path of undo.
Twigs do not snap, here where nobody can hear –
tread less gently, my floret.

The woods will not swallow you whole unless
your bones are softer than June.

And this shelter has always been here? Awaiting
my whey face?

The branches have been just begging for you. Dearest,
twitch your big teeth – cleave my hand and use
it to brush the white sand from your hair.

Christening

I set my ribs out in front of me; play operas
while you sweep. Put down your otherness, love,
that makes my head a vertigo:
pass me the knitting and let us conjoin.
We whittle hours away making broths, gathering
hordes of flowers that I wade through
to thrust fresh marigolds into your arms.

I try to homemake a happiness. I keep
stocks of lemon and sugar: season artichoke
lungs and hearts. I hold your hand as if
it could be dropped, carefully clean
the dirt from your nails.

He is good to me, in ways,
I tell my mother when she calls. He helps cook,
helps weave; covers me in leaves so I am not cold.

Hold the gaps between my fingers; the rivulets
holding my sanity in my head: help
me flicker and wither into the frail thing
you can store in the hollows of your body.

I am sorry, but I am love-starved and lonely. I have
crawled continent lengths searching for resonance:
invented bodies that aren't there.

Arterial

Carcasses glisten when you tell them you love them.
They float and glow and grow stupid.
What I would do to rouse game, for you, all
summer: to alcove under your tongue.

My ribs, my spine, the tiny   bone in my
tiniest toe: I give to you to build cages.
I fold and dissolve as I try my hardest
to become   something you can hold as half divine.

I want to turn yellow for you and grow calm.
 Have everything you love poured over you
                like a flood of sparkling sea foam.

You suggest I be walked; I   knock
on your front teeth and crawl into your mouth.
We weave ruddy paths, eyes hungry for warmer
bodies. I hear screams before limbs
fall on to me. One with the piercing chorus,
I   push them down your throat.

Floating

When I was young, my mother would say
'до свадьбы заживет'. Roughly, *'It will heal
before your wedding.' Oh, but if she could see me now,
with an entire body decaying.*

You clot in my left artery, until complicity
is folding stray animal traps into the batter: baking
cakes from the ache and the oats.
*Do you mean all the soft whisperings that you
have been sending to me like a dream?*
I take on your aberrations as my own: put in
blind eyes when you are at murder.

Pressing plums and juniper into your wine,
I sate my ache biting off honeyed flesh: teeth
imprints on the skins: light   dustings of powdered
sugar giving away where I have wept.

Bury your chilling hands under the slits
in my skin; the warm red I am shedding
regardless. My flesh falls from my bones:
we add to the stew and find a new pelt.

Liquid Fingernails

You skin the rabbit till the moon is cold. Oh,
how sweet the summers used to be while I
was not punctured by the eldritch, and kept.

But some hands hold you to eat you.
Some hearts blue and coated in tar:
that thread through your head and lasso you.

Old turnip, full to the liver of flattery, I sleep now
in a huge cradle of a house, rocking
irrespective of winds. My head rests upon
a hundred others, severed so cleanly my hair is

not spotted. Apricots dry among slivers of skin;
sparrow guts litter my bedroom.

Cut me open and locusts take flight.
  Chip   at the begging and find bones
     set wrong; tissue and bone straining
   to be buried among   warm bodies.

Borderling

In the temple of soft twigs, the fresh   skins of
our bodies   ceasefire; over ants, over
grass-wisps, over wine.   We pool
our spoils together,   heads stuffy with
the scent of orchids; the redolence splitting away
and pulling us closer together. My hair to my ankles
surrendered to your scissors; would have
    shrouded us like the sea.

I was going easy on the first hundred.
But now, I must have slaughter; half mad
rabbits kneeling before me,   skin
    scrubbed raw post-killing.

Naïf

You cannot flee abhorrence if it follows you.   If it
    screams in your ear for more pheasant and pooling
cream: turns to a wolf with fangs that   spin
a   spiralling chrysalis from the lamplight.

    Phantoms folded into the darkness
  whisper   up from beneath rotting leaves.
I hear faint screaming always: cannot sleep but
dream of floorboards peeling up: voices
    singing   of silver-skeined afterlife.

The wolf says: be careful of your open eyes: I
am hungry for glistening apples.

The wolf says: shall we retire together?
I have been waiting for a rabbit born red.

Vous Serez Ma Proie

But there is carnage, love or no love.
Claws jutting out of soft skin;
raw claws that know how to bite – teeth
that think   for you, *mon amour,* for you
I have done   this mercy.   Endured the
crypt of a withering love: a crypt that
   winds around itself until we   are seeds in the
pit of a soulless feeding: until everything is all that
  it seems.   His softness swallows you whole.

Did you wish to see a sea that looks like wine?
There is no delusion strong enough to mask
the choking stench of roses: the dead bodies
they hide and take care of.

How do I grow kinder bones? How
do I cradle these ruptured bodies – stop
twisting faces and repent?

Mon petit chou

We eat the hearts first, most times.
    Sharing, treasure two chambers
  each, swimming with squash and pale
juice. Of course, to begin,

          joints were difficult. Tonight,
    tomorrow, they slip apart like
toads perpetually wet;   oiled sparrows
keen to take flight.   Arms? Severed logs
      in our fire.

On dark days, I reconstruct skeletons;
hang   up tinkling windchimes.   When

birds   catch in the ribs (poor
    babies – poor rattling)   *of course,*
my edelweiss crown.   *Of course I did this*
    for you.

Atropa Belladonna

What am I to do with all the dead birds I can't hold?
  They overspill like liquid twilight
    grown sentient: seeping over homes and into
gutters like   pale, periwinkle waves.

I never dreamt I could harbour such corruption: coax it
into young beaks and not care. But spines plucked out
     become bows for you   to hunt anew:
        you reduce my marrow on the stove.

I feel rather like a fish. Rather like
    the bad man your grandmother warned you of
when she told you not to visit the woods:
   the woods that devour you entire
          and leave a pile of clothes at the door.

Over-Adequate

New-born hearts flitter up to adorn my hair;
their veins, halcyon bracelets.
We drown in this forest together;
stumbling hand-held into a timeless dream
where again, and again, we are sacrificed.
Crisis lodges in my bones as innate; I cannot
talk but gasp up paranoia and post-larcenic guilt;
clotting blood,   wild orchids quivering.

'oft are one – the murderer and victim.
'oft are one – th' innocent floret and serpent under't
    'oft are   one – the black air and hot soot
    shoved in my lungs - crass taxidermic noon-mares

Your heart – oh, how it shines like the apple
seen in the mirrors of my dreams!

Viridis

When the light is just right stray rabbits
   see a cottage, resting on glinting
straw. When night falls and mirages shift,
     our poor cottage is a haven against
ghosts that paw at the door.

Discarnate   wailings fly up to hide
     in the clouds: spit down
   aurin droplets of rain, red and round-bodied,

all for us, this testing of guilt and repent.
   Needle threaded, I sew larger
leaves into umbrellas; wavering,
     with leather-skins, hide.

Forest Bathing

Orphan, go long. Tell   all
    for five wisps of a glance: hold
the shivering   like it is forgivable.   Did I
    ever tell you of the tears that fell

down the young pianist's face;
    turning to pearls as they gathered in weight?
        Distress   is the extreme agony and ache
  that occurs when you realise your   blood

        is not peppered with starlings.
How   do I

Fairy tales

You crawled out of the sea, hazy thing;
    straining   for the wispy-blue turrets.
  There is no strength in the whey-face to halt

   your approach;   you reach my parents with
ease. The sky   falling over you

   is only my desire; the fatal net on an
early night   already cold.

But now is not the time. Now   is
    the time for raising the red flag and wailing:
    for escaping the   sad sirens that   try
        to rescue / capture /   eat me
  and spin up all of the blue   for themselves.

     You are of the worst,
you   darling of the sea, that lives   with the killers and
   crabs;

        this castle   is all foam and no substance.

   Don't tell me to smile and eat up.
      It came in a dream, it came on a cloud –   pray,
    stop this fey-tale -   I am tired   of eyes
soaked in rust.

Crab-Fishing

I have been all day baking bread for you: hoping
we can put our knives to better use. I toy
with stuffing it into the   cracks of our castle
so we   cannot   be reached by the sad wailings of
     the sea.   My love, let

the hollow thing not want for love,
  Not   want for endless bowls   of fresh skin:
I have been beached and waiting for years.

I have been sat here dreaming redress. Gargling
barnacles to tell my family I cannot come.

Nothing is to be Mine; Everything Ours

Every rat and stray sea-girl brought clams and fresh lace: every dark corner was covered in mirrors. A thousand young brides beamed, a thousand dew drops collected in gold bathtubs, a thousand woodland guests ate mushrooms soaked in cream and drank fig-juice from egg-shell goblets. I did not eat, let alone kill, anything that once had a face. In the downy, pastel air that glinted with fleeting moments of gold, the quaint bodies seemed suspended: to be drunken with felicity, only a whisper away from floating: knocking heads among the clouds and bitter stars.

We split a fresh maiden in half. My portion is still lodged in our chimney flute: even then, I could not meet her eyes. We promised our livers and hearts to each other, made rings from withering squid. My shoes were then still spun of clean ivory, and the blushing days did not dissolve so rapidly into ghastly, huckleberry nights.

My hutch sat waiting in the corner. One hand carried wild dandelions as the other kept hold of my dress, pretending I could not see my cage open and close; shift continuously closer. *Please,* my eyes would implore. *Please, you do not mean that for me?*

Mère Vampire

Come, my little cabbage that mirrors me
exactly. Help me fashion a cot in this cottage
that has before you seen only death.

I have locked up the bad men in their coffins:
called the cobbler to give you new feet.

Do you see, in the moth-light, how
my bones are beginning to warm? How the baby
stars are still fragile and not yet upset:
how my claws retract to hold you.

We can bathe in fondness and clotted cream. Watch
parades of ducks and capture your favourite goose
so she is never boiled into soup.

Mère mal

But visiting flocks upset the salt and I
am forced to inflate your friends, like fish,
and tie them up. You find me green-faced
under macabre balloons and I try to explain -
I poured all my peace into your frame.

Come morning, I open mouth to apologise –
a toad bleats and falls out. Looking down, up
for an explanation I see only my baby's
vicious eyes. I try again – a rat; serpent,
baby mole – *Non, mon bébé lapin –*
you have not muted your mother?

Alice

Fall back in to your flesh, though pounded and
   raw, it might be. Roll   back those
mismatched eyes   until
      the rattling things   hit jackpot;
   both tender gold, glittering things
        any fresh bride should wear.

But do you think I can shed my red fur? Spin
flaxen hair into gold? Oh,
twin body, so far we have walked
with nothing but clovers on our feet.
Mirror friend – if you shatter, will your
Streaky heart
        be free to elope with me?

Ephialtes

Look! The moon is not watching! Let us
frolic and press wine – overflow our goblets
with figs and star-sap; crumble up
biscuits we have only just baked
so the birds grow bigger than their nests.
Stay with me, stay with me, dear darling.
Heart-hurt has sat heavy on my back
since I wed: *shed, like a snake- oh, and*
perhaps I shall! Be rid of this blue
and vile worm!

I ration out the left chambers of my heart,
sat among soft soil   up-tousled with waking
bodies. Sundays spent rousing corpses
with soft nudges; with a gentle, almond mouth –
oh, to shake with the stars as they do when chill hits.
Poor babies of my garden, there is no water, no
feed – only digging, only want.

Your darkness, caressing me so softly
I do not notice whole layers slipping off.

Stockholm

My darling, is this not enough?
I have sat and woven cages for you to trap your lovers:
I have fooled them into thinking I am safe.
Darling, delivering the *coup de grâce* myself
was not a choice; I lay upon you all innocence.

I was never warned of the dark, cooing things
that know how to crawl and delude. Little
flecks   of softening crawl under my skin and
 in my heart, take root.

Of course you can have my eyes.
Of course   you can whittle my bones into an ornate
     cage that can hold me safe: hold me
as an aureate thing.

Your fingers start to feel for the weak parts
of my throat. A chalice, idle and ready to collect
   the pathetic thing that folds. My nails
catch as I climb in: My mother watches
        through the ocean and screams.

Red Lettuce

I am not mad, yet
            yet I stir up the mud and make pancakes
for my squirrels: my skin, by now, is too thin.
All the faults of my heart (how cold it is;
how pathetic) – why, I am anaemic and must need blood.
Diagnosis strung   in my bow, I shoot pigeons and
         badgers: steal their blood and drink up.

My body, by now, is stranger. I
catch sight in the pooling and pause.
A limp suit of skin, bloodied and hung
up to dry like a dress, is left of the once-upon.

The lungs in our garden have started
   to sprout – I spatter them   like pumpkins.
Moon-framed, I bury evidence among the
radishes, bitten   raw by odd bugs that know

what I have done.   Crawl over to a chain of paper
girls and   ask politely if they can hide me   and
the fury is coming in so hold me, small angels: help me.

I was so young I still cared for liquorice. So desperate
I crammed berries and bees into my mouth: tried
to displace my decay into a daughter.

Chorus

Sorrow this, sorrow that –
Child, you have grown wanton and wild.

Do you not hear the women wailing out for you?
Your cup overspilleth, indeed, but there is no glory in a crown
fashioned from the threads of your children.

Unholy, unmotherly lady snaking through our houses,
murdering men and stealing the heads of our young;

bold shadow of Medea, called mother – straighten out
your sorrowful husband, feasting on spitted flesh.

Bloodlines

Oyster teacup that frails on my lip,
that catches my tears in its chip.
I promise, it is only wine.
Chisels come for my skin. On the floor,
my porcelain face quite loses its charm;

its pieces swim among the ants and call hither.
Oh, but I am lonely – so
covered in toothpicks and garlic.

There is no monster that doesn't soften
with love. No inky figure that doesn't wish
for a body to rise from the woods;
to remember its birthday and sing to it.

Suivez-Moi. Je Vous Attendais.

But I am no longer sane, my lover:
I sleep and I dream of the salt in your blood
collecting and slicing at the seams.
I wake and dream of being enshrined
in a cage made up of your limbs:
weaving a blanket for you from my hair.
Feeding you figs and the bones of your birds –
My darling, here are my fingers.

My teeth are the only bones I can offer you
in public: I smile till my cheeks lure in
old leeches.

Take it, from my mouth – all the
honey I have spent months trying to trick
into staying; the night-hours spent
wishing I was peaceful in slumber.

Lore

It is said that if you leave out a loaf for the couple in the woods, your hearth is spared from harm. That once, the young girl had eyes gentler than carnations that rise in midsummer; that she would pull all morning at lute strings for wild rabbits; grow lemons for them even through winter. Light would break through the pollen floating atop her head: soft, incandescent splits of pale colour that rebounded on glassy eyes. It is said that these forests were pleasant. Elegant stalks entwined with the glinting notes of her song, and were only outshone by leaking stars.

And now, alas, we find crowns of little toe-bones littered among our rhubarb. Any child that strays will be soft spoken with tones of saffron into a haze of almost-sleep; severed at the neck, hair rushing from the blade like cascades of golden worm silk.

Blink, and the cottage sprouts into a castle: look away, it buckles to an abattoir. Like dewy lettuce leaves folding back, the delusions arrest and run away from us in turn. Some bodies fall prey, some wear crystalline bluebells instead of their eyes, so they are not led by whispers into the sparkling sea; the red twig-palace covered in pelts. The trees grow, out of fear, in straight rows. It is said, to the young girls overcome with berry-cheeks, *'Much better stay spinster than marry a tyrant. Just look at the halfwit in the woods.'*

Feral in the Woods

You've locked me in my hutch, so I sit
stirring patterns into salt on the floor, threading
heads of sailors together on a necklace that I
will shrink down and wear to our dinners.

You have made sure there is no one for miles.
My love, have you hidden the knives? You know I
see through you like an oracle. The eggs

pile up in a pyramid, infinitely threatening
to engulf us. You know they never hatch –
not after all the frog feet roasted for bunting;
all the gallons we have shed and soaked up.
You crack one open and hand me my tongue.

We are not so different, these days.
We have learnt how to eat and be eaten.
Except I, in my old age of only perhaps two decades,
have grown irreparably tired.

Metamorpho

Monarchs flutter about her shoulders; encircle her head and follow her – loyal friends, throughout these years. She places the hare in the oven, throws the cat in the sink, and scrubs turnips till they are as raw as her hands. At noon, she will bat away the cobwebs and chase out the mice: she will study her face in her spoon. Slowly, shuddering like the baby robin waiting to see if the water is warm, she will turn herself inside out. Her husband is coming to dinner.

Marcid

Being brutal is no easy feat. I paint myself
horrific and draw blood; spit poison darts
at fresh babies. In the elsewhere, soft-winged seraphim

are humming and floating atop velvet fruits
and the night draws only true charm from
their veins. It feeds a thousand stretches of
skin; turns half carmine and half
luminescent – I croak and start to collapse.

Dark things do not itch for malice from birth.
I have long wanted to dig up my corpses; with
ivory needles, weave spindly apologies through their spines.

Choking

Tell me where to put the anger.
Tell me where to put the heart breaking.

You Can't Shoot Ten Rabbits At Once

Learn to swim, learn to carve:
stuff our hearts with blunt hope
and I eat you. My love –

am I yet full enough of the bitter,
poisonous things you have been
feeding me for our supper?

I dream only of being adored. Of you
growing kind fingers made of soft leaves;
a blanket that does not pin me down.

Verdure

Alone, with you left sleeping in late May, the poor
apples fail to grow and the almonds stay scratching
at their jars. Barefoot, dewy grass flattens for
my path. The sky, an unfurling wash of violet
peaches, makes soft the water I walk to.

Nymph-insects wait always in the grass, whispering
to you where I move. Over time I have tamed them
with cheese: pricked their vanity with endless flattery.

And how lovely to lay under skies shot through
with milk scorned and spat out by
baby angels; the petals they have shed
from their crowns. The frogs collect on me
like a lily leaf: a refuge somehow adrift. Elden stars,
likewise plagued with the guilt of shooting, peer
down and send blushing blankets of air:
downy whispers of effervescent love.

I come home to an oven full of children. A husband
so full of hemlock he is still knocked out.

Tossing

My darling, how well can you float? Because
    lately I've been growing disillusioned and
soft: I sit looking at the cages with remorse.
  I wish   to be remembered in hues of pale gold:
    in tones   of tenderness and pink.

I am naïve, but not quite liquid. I have seen you fashioning
 my spider friends   into little drops of
  crystallised sugar   that will delude and choke me into
staying. I cannot tell which you are   more eager for;
    which of my limbs you would most like to frame.

Entr'acte

In another world, I have already killed you.
 We no longer weave crowns and play Gods;
     I show my   Teeth and wade through the smothering.
I emancipate; I dissociate; I   pin your heart to the wall and

stare.   I close my eyes and you still slightly shine.
My gold lovely, so made of softness I
   was too scared to take you near corners: too
       in awe to see keen edges.

My heart has seen less dire days.   Are we
        not sick of carting around   this mangled thing; of
pressing wine in barrels littered with glass

    when we could be almond-dancing and
        stretching up towards the stars   alone?

Mother

You came from a dream in the night.
   I have guarded you like a garnet ever since.

Wishes

I've been dreaming of the sun and white clothes.
Of an endless garden of opening hearts:
visiting peace that untangles my hair.
I yield tender hands, offer strawberries
unharmed – I dissolve in the blushing air
and wear thin voices perched on
flitting glass. I feel a new tongue taking shape.

It is just the right night for the stars
to swim through the water; play tag, play
catch; surround the stray violets and columbines.

I have been dreaming of a heart that knows piano.
Of a conscience that loves me better.

Cleaved, Softening Beaks

I do not want to make musical sounds.

There Is No Such Thing As Soft Violence

We are older, now.
I remember your cages and branches.
Moonlit burials dart behind my eyes:
I remember your glint and your thieving.
I carry guilt still around like a baby: slippery thing
I cannot lose, though I am so dismantled
there are thousands of gaps.

Will you play catch with me, old lover?
You are grown weak in your old age:
grown forgetful of those you tricked
into your forest of withering.

Let us have so much wine that we choke.
Enough apricots and honey and crystallised figs
that our fingers stain with the opulence.

The grass has not stopped growing since you sat.
It folds round   like an evening that is
   sick of being lucid: envelops you.
I take firm hold of your ribs and   pull.

I Have a Pain in Our Teeth

Cornered, I swallow your body and with it,
  moulding remains. You nestle in my stomach

and build shelter,   hide from hunters, cry   up
through my   throat for wine, blood –   comforts

that keep you plump. I carry and tend to you like
      mother: you make me retch and grow sallow.

Defiance grows slow, in bodies almost
translucent.   Bones milked and hardened, cup

  emptied   of sorrow, I drink yew berries mixed
in with milk.   When you are not looking,

I bathe you in lemon juice   carefully cursed:
  oh, a nettle, for a towel. You have   taught

     your young bride which fungi are toxic: I make
  soup, I make pie, I sear them with   garlic and thyme.
You unrest, writhe – grow ill as I did when I ate you.

I bury in a frenzy of squawking birds: your screaming,
married to theirs.
I sit and I carve out the rot.

Godnonsensical

Hera,   Hera,

    Hera,

             Mother,

    Hera,   goddess

    OH - - what is this evil?

Arcadia

You have always had two faces. Consumed
and exhumed, I bind your doll-body in twine:
kiss each eyelid, fold the first flowers
you ever gave me into your hair. I
circumference your face with a knife.
I would rather skin clementines than peel
back your features, but *oh* -
Electra of the heavens has unleashed the taps:
I float on the gold of heaven's rain.

Stunned, silenced for a throat full of bliss,
I tip your shadow into the river. I wash
bloodstains from osier shirts: fold stars
and flute-notes in with my linens.

If (he be) alive, may the sea foam milk
If (he be) dead, may the sea foam blood

The Sea-Foam Crown

She emerged a dread-wraith in day-break, cloaked in such gallons of blood we thought a thousand rabbits must have seen slaughter; such majesty every throat constricted. Skinned red grape; dead maiden of our tales, she sprouted florets never-browning. Rotten seeds, underfoot, effloresced and blossomed. Her hair, a halo of tumbling waves, sat sanguine pillow to the lilies we tossed atop it.

Sea foam erupted and turned to wine. *Oh Mary*, we cried, *You have returned! You have freed your daughter from the ground.* Trees politely uprooted. Buck-skins scattered; doe ghosts rose with young girls from the ground – souls made wholly of milk. We collapsed to our knees as red shrouding melted; grew aureate and pearlescent.

She arrested from inside out. Organs and entrails flared under a transparent, rice paper chest; freshly-boiled blood clotted into rubies. Her liver nibbled up all the rot. Layers of sullied skin lifted in ribbons, spinning about her like streamers; forked tongues wove about her wrists. Delirious, dreaming, we raised her on our shoulders and emptied gardens for her adulation. Faceless, drowning, we poured the earliest rays of summer warmth into her mouth.

To Glow

Little voices tread water; float up
like dead bodies determined to be found.

They whisper; *Are you moon-struck?*
Are you drunk? No, my starlings:

I am happy and there is no cause.
I swim and I lily-dance; my fingers
cradle egg-shells that never break.

My hands are soft and made only of honey.
I bathe in oil and my scars luminesce.

In ten decades, perhaps, I will blush
to uncurl among paradise. For now,
I knit my pet rabbits small jumpers.
I sway with the willows and drink from oranges.

www.ingramcontent.com/pod-product-compliance
Lightning Source LLC
Chambersburg PA
CBHW051809100526
44592CB00016B/2628